Book Power
Year 2

Literacy through Literature

Jane Bunting, Sue Ellis, Jenny Vernon

clpe
Centre for Literacy
in Primary Education

ISBN 978-1-872267-46-3

© Copyright 2010

Centre for Literacy in Primary Education
Webber Street
London SE1 8QW
Telephone: 020 7401 3382/3
info@clpe.co.uk
www.clpe.co.uk

CLPE is an independent Charitable Trust
Registered Charity No. 1092698
Registered Company No. 04385537

Contents

Introducing the key teaching approaches
Using texts as the core of a literacy programme

The children's books featured in this book all lend themselves to being talked and thought about in depth in the Year Two classroom. They have been chosen because they are powerful stories which are likely to engage children, stir their ideas and feelings and involve them in discussion.

Each book is the focus of a unit of work that lasts for two to six weeks providing opportunities for a wide range of work in literacy. Working in this way means that children can get to know a book really well.

The approaches suggested here are designed to enable children to respond to the books more intensively and to reflect on them in a variety of ways including talk and writing. In addition young writers learn a lot about writing from their reading and can use these texts as a starting point and inspiration for their own writing.

Reading aloud

Reading aloud is arguably the most important thing that teachers can do and needs to be a frequent and regular part of each school day.

Reading aloud slows written language down so that children can hear and take in the tunes and patterns of it. It enables children to experience and enjoy stories they might otherwise not meet. By reading well-chosen books aloud, teachers help classes to become communities of readers. As such they can share in experiences of a wide repertoire of books they enjoy and get to know well. Subsequent conversations about books help children to explore and reflect on stories in ways that are made meaningful, personal and pleasurable.

Before reading a book to a class, teachers should read it for themselves: in this way they can think about the best way to read it. If children are to respond to the tunes and the meanings of a book it needs to be read aloud in a way that engages the listener.

Re-reading

Opportunities for re-reading a book that they have previously listened to helps all children to engage more deeply with it. Reading and re-reading known texts is very important for all readers, but particularly for less experienced readers or those for whom English is an additional language as it helps make the text more familiar and enables them to read it for themselves with more confidence.

Three important times for children to revisit books are during shared reading, group reading and independent reading. Teachers are encouraged to include all of these in these units because they provide supported opportunities to extend conversations about the books.

Responding and reflecting

The following approaches help children to respond to the questions:

How do you like this book?
What does it make you think/feel?
What do you think it all means?

They encourage children to reflect on the meanings of the text that they are reading, to recognise and explore their own responses to it and to begin to develop their understanding of what the writer has to say.

Booktalk

Discussion about books forms the foundations for working around texts. Children need frequent, regular and sustained opportunities to talk together about the books that they are reading as a whole class. The more experience they have of talking together like this the better they get at making explicit the meanings that a text holds for them: a child quoted in Aidan Chambers' book *Tell Me: Children, Reading & Talk* says 'we don't know what we think about a book until we've talked about it'.

This booktalk is supportive to all readers and writers, but it is especially empowering for children who find literacy difficult. It helps the class as a whole to reach shared understandings and move towards a more dispassionate debate of ideas and issues.

In this book we offer suggestions for the sorts of questions that teachers and children might use in discussion. These questions are shown in italics.

Asking the basic questions - getting the talk started

Once they have heard a book read aloud, the class can begin to explore their response to it with the help of what Chambers calls the four basic questions. These questions give children accessible starting points for discussion:

Tell me…was there anything you liked about this book?
Was there anything that you particularly disliked..?
Was there anything that puzzled you?
Were there any patterns…any connections that you noticed…?

The openness of these questions unlike the more interrogative 'Why?' question encourages every child to feel that they have something to say, and allows everyone to take part in arriving at a shared view.

As children reply it can be useful to write down what they say under the headings 'likes', 'dislikes', 'puzzles', 'patterns'. This written record helps to map out the class's view of the important meanings and is a way of holding on to ideas for later.

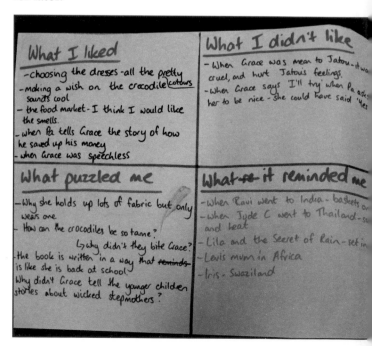

This is an especially useful way to begin working on a new story or book and will lead children inevitably into a fuller discussion using more general and focussed questions. Once children are used to working with the 'Tell me' questions they can use them for themselves when talking about their reading with each other.

Asking the 'special' questions

'Tell me' also contains suggestions for 'special' questions to use once discussion has taken off. These are questions which direct children's attention more closely to themes or ideas that are particularly important to an understanding of the story but which might otherwise be overlooked.

Reading journals

Both class and individual reading journals provide a thinking space for children to explore and reflect on their reading experience through writing and drawing.

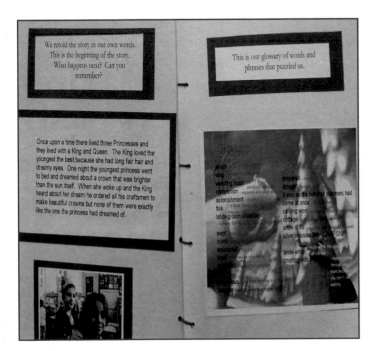

Interpreting and performing

The following key teaching approaches help children to interpret the meanings that the text holds for them, using a variety of expressive means including dance, music and art.

They help children to answer the questions:

What kind of meanings does this story/poem have for you?
How can we bring out these meanings for others?

Storytelling and re-telling

Re-telling a story is a powerful way for children to make a story their own. Storytelling helps children concentrate on the best way to tell the story and to make deliberate choices about the words and phrases they use in the telling. All of this will help greatly when they come to writing.

When a story is familiar it is easier for a reader to get hold of its shape, and to consider how it fits together. Children can use storyboards or story maps as supports for their re-telling. These techniques help them identify the 'bones' of the story. Longer stories can be 'passed around' a story circle; children build confidence by telling a small part of the story and then passing it on to the next person.

Role-play and drama

Role-play and drama provide immediate routes into the world of a story and allow children to explore texts actively. They enable children to put themselves into a particular character's shoes and imagine how things would look from that point of view. Through drama and role-play children can imagine characters' body language, behaviour and tones of voice, in ways that they can draw on later when they write.

Freeze-frame

Freeze-frames are still images or tableaux. They can be used to enable groups of children to examine a key event or situation from a story and decide in detail how it could be represented. When presenting the freeze-frame, one of the group could act as a commentator to talk through what is happening in their version of the scene, or individual characters could be asked to speak their thoughts out loud.

Hot seating

In hot seating, one of the class role-plays a key character from a poem or story and is interviewed by the rest. This activity involves children in examining a character's motivation closely. Before the hot seating, children need to discuss what they want to know in order to identify questions and ideas that they want answering. If children have no experience of hot seating the teacher may initially need to take on the role.

Writing in role

When children have explored a fictional situation through talk or role-play they may be ready to write in role as a character in a story. Taking the role of a particular character enables even very young writers to see events from that viewpoint and involves them in writing in a different voice. In role, children can often access feelings and language that are not available to them when they write as themselves.

Performing poetry

All poetry needs to be lifted off the page and given voice. Whether they are reading or writing poetry it helps if children work with performance in mind. Children invited to prepare poems for performance may choose to enliven them by using a rhythmic or musical accompaniment to the words.

Visualising

Asking children to picture or to 'visualise' a character or place from a story is a way of encouraging them to move into a fictional world. Children can be asked to picture the scene in their mind's eye or 'walk around it' in their imagination. Once they have done so, they can bring it to life by describing it in words or recreating it in drawing or painting.

This is a way for children to begin to articulate their response to what they read and can help children to analyse the ways in which the writer has used language and images to create a world.

Drawing and annotating
Opportunities to draw before and during writing increase young children's motivation, and can help them to think. Drawing can help all writers plan their writing and develop their ideas.

Drawing and annotating settings
Drawing story settings prompts children to imagine what a scene looks like, or visualise it from a particular viewpoint.

Drawing and annotating characters
Drawing characters focuses attention on them - how they look, what they say, how they behave. To support their idea of what a character is like children have to refer to the text. They can also be encouraged to draw on the language of the text in making annotations around the drawings.

Responding to illustration
All of the books have been chosen because of the quality of the illustrations they contain and the ways in which the illustrations work with the text to create meaning for the reader. Children will need time and opportunity to enjoy and respond to the pictures and to talk together about what they contribute to their understanding of the texts. There could be opportunities for children to develop their responses by drawing or painting in a similar style to the illustrations.

Illustrating the text
Opportunities to illustrate a story during an activity such as bookmaking give children the chance to draw on the ideas that they have gained from talk, storymaking, role-play and drawing. They enable children to engage in creative re-interpretations of the text.

Shared writing
Shared writing is possibly the most important way a teacher can help all children to experience what it's like to be a writer.

Acting as scribe the teacher works with a group of children to create a text together. Teacher and children work as active partners, talking together to share ideas while the teacher guides the children through all the decisions that writers need to make and helps them shape their thoughts on paper.

Shared writing gives children a model for their own independent writing and results in clear literary outcomes such as a poster, Big Book or poem that everyone can enjoy.

Bookmaking
Publishing their work for an audience helps children to write more purposefully. Bookmaking provides a motivating context within which children can bring together their developing understandings of what written language is like; making written language meaningful as they construct their own texts. The decisions that all writers have to take and the processes of redrafting, editing and punctuation can be demonstrated and discussed as teachers and children write together in shared writing.

Re-enactment through play
Revisiting stories through a range of play-based experiences helps children to step into the world that someone else has created and to explore it more completely.

Role-play areas
Linking the role-play area to a known story provides important opportunities for children to get inside the story. As they play the story it helps them to understand its structure, allows them to put themselves into a character's shoes and to think, talk and behave like that character. It

encourages them to experiment with the 'what if' of the plot and make it their own. If the role-play area is set up with the children's help they will be involved in thinking about the detail of this fictional world, in making decisions about what this world should be like, and in illuminating it with their own experience.

Small world play

Opportunities for small world play that are based on a known story promote talk about the shape of the story, encourage children to discuss key elements such as character and plot and to make decisions about how they create the setting. As they play, whether as individuals or in cooperation with others, they practise their narrative skills and 'try on' the different characters using different voices to bring them to life.

Story boxes

Story boxes create opportunities to revisit and develop the themes and storylines of a particular story. Typically, they consist of a shoebox containing a range of small toys and inspirational objects. The box itself can be turned into a setting for the story using a variety of collage materials and with sides cut to fold down. However, the box is at its most effective when something intriguing or unexpected is added. Children can use the box to storytell the next episode of a story or create another story with a similar setting or characters.

Exploring and analysing text

This section features the key teaching approaches that aim to help children to think about the questions:

How does this text work?
How is it made?

When exploring a story in terms of its language and structure and how these contribute to its meanings, it is important to build on children's spontaneous interest in language and plan investigative work around it.

The approaches that follow help children pay close attention to aspects of the way the text is shaped, and consider individual and specific features of plot, structure or language.

Mapping

Mapping a story and its setting helps to develop a sense of the story world.

Maps of story settings

Mapping story settings is a way of establishing the geography of a story more securely and visualising where its characters and events would be located. These kinds of maps can be drawn by pairs, groups, individuals, or by the teacher, drawing on a flip chart or interactive whiteboard to construct a map or plan where characters and events of the story can be located.

Story maps

Making a story map is a way of re-telling the story. It is a graphic means of breaking a story down into episodes and sequencing its events. This kind of graphic representation helps children to hold on to the shape of the story more confidently so that they can re-tell it orally or in writing. Children can also make story maps as a form of planning, to prepare for their own writing.

Storyboards

A storyboard is another way of helping to map out key scenes in the story through drawing and annotation. Originally used to plot scenes in film or moving picture work it is particularly useful for marking out the key scenes in a story within a given number of frames (usually 6 or 8), or for focussing in on the next few moments in a sequence.

Drawing up comparison charts

A comparison grid is a visual way of recording similarities or differences in style, language or content, for example when considering the question:

How is this version of the story like that one?

Talking together as a whole class about how you might collect 'evidence' in this kind of way helps children to see patterns in texts. A chart could help with comparing story beginnings or looking at different characters.

Debate and argument

Talking together about books following the 'Tell me' questions is a very powerful way to explore and reflect on emotional response to a story and what it means for us as individuals. In contrast, debating ideas calls for a more formal and objective response to the story and helps children begin to analyse how the writer has made us feel this way.

Teachers can structure debates inviting 'for' and 'against' arguments around particular statements arising from a book.

Looking at language

Text-marking

In text-marking children are asked to highlight particular lines or words that they like from the story they are reading and to say what it is they like about them in particular. In the beginning the teacher will want to demonstrate this as a whole class activity modelling the ways in which children might respond and the sort of reflective comment they might use before asking children to work in groups to focus on the language in a similar way.

Word Collections

The making of word collections is a way of focusing on the language of a story or poem. Children could make collections of words that describe a particular character's feelings, or they can collect words that describe a place or situation. Collecting words in this way helps children to have a more focused awareness of the ways language affects our perceptions and understandings of character and the ways in which the author creates the readers' response.

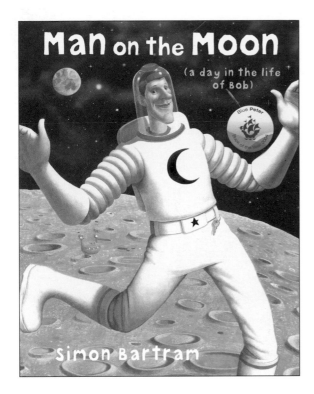

Man on the Moon
(a day in the life of Bob)
Simon Bartram

A teaching sequence of 3 to 4 weeks

Learning aims

- To explore, develop and sustain ideas by talking, listening and responding to others' contributions

- To provide children with a stimulating and meaningful writing context for a range of purposes

- To empathise and engage with characters through role-play and writing

- To help children discover that words and pictures can tell stories in different ways

- To use a fictional text as a starting point for work across the curriculum

This original book, with its striking illustrations and gentle humour is a great favourite with children and adults alike. Bob's routine existence, his dated yet homely décor and Fair Isle tank top contrast absurdly with his exotic day job as janitor and tour guide on the moon. Accompanying him on his surreal daily journey to the moon, observing him at work where he entertains the moon tourists, tidies up after them and switches on the moon's night light before returning home to his evening bath and cocoa, the reader becomes aware that the illustrations and the text are telling two different stories.

The parallel story is introduced early on through a spectacular double-page spread depicting quirky green creatures lurking in the moon's craters. While Bob emphatically reassures us that there is no such thing as aliens, careful scrutiny reveals these little creatures peeking out everywhere.

Young readers are delighted to be part of this gradually unfolding conspiracy about which Bob seems oblivious.

Key Teaching Approaches

Booktalk

Shared writing

Drama

Drawing and annotation

Visualising

Class journal

Bookmaking

Writing in role

Drawing and annotating

Research and information writing

Before beginning this unit of work:

This book fits very well with a topic on space. With the children's help give your reading area a space theme, displaying a range of related information books and setting up a moon souvenir shop. The book also provides strong links with art and design, DT and maths.

Session one:

Booktalk

Prepare a class journal made from large sheets of sugar paper stapled together to capture the children's responses and examples of their work as you progress through the teaching sequence.

Without showing the front cover of the book, introduce Bob by displaying the image of him in his front room. Take care to cover the text first so that the children respond only to the picture. Divide the class into four groups, giving each group a specific focus to discuss in relation to the image:

What does the picture remind you of?
Would you like to meet Bob? Give reasons for your choice.
What do you think Bob's hobbies might be?
What would you like to know about Bob?

Ask each group to respond in turn and invite the class to ask questions or to make comments, stressing that there is no right or wrong answer. Scribe the children's responses around the image, labelling any clues they find about Bob and his hobbies.

Put the children into groups of four to discuss what they would like to ask Bob and ask them to note these questions down onto post-its. After discussion list their queries on a prepared grid in

the class journal for future reference. Using shared writing compose a class letter to Bob and 'post' it along with all the post-its to him.

Session two:

Reading aloud and booktalk

Prepare an envelope containing the book and a letter from Bob thanking the class for their interesting questions and saying that he has sent the book by way of an explanation. After briefly reviewing the class questions, read the book aloud, asking the children to listen for any information that helps answer their questions. Take feedback from this discussion, noting it down in the class journal. Put the children into pairs to identify their favourite parts of the story. Ask them to give the reasons for their choices and then to share these ideas with whole class. There will doubtless be an animated discussion about the aliens. You can discuss with the children the ways in which the author shares a secret with them to which Bob is not privy and how this contributes to their enjoyment of the story.

Ask the children to sketch and annotate their favourite scene from the story. Add these to the class journal.

Session three:

Drama and drawing

Show the children some real illustrations of the moon in addition to the ones in the book. Discuss what they think it might be like to walk on the moon, what potential hazards there might be such as craters and whether there might be any moon beings or animals. Re read the story up to the part where the moon tourists arrive. In the hall or a large space, organise the children in pairs explaining that one child will be Bob, and the other a moon tourist. Ask all the children who are in role as Bob to take the tourists on a guided tour of the moon. This involves leading their partners, who have their eyes closed, by the finger tip, describing the setting and pointing out all the sights, sounds, smells and obstacles as they proceed. Change roles after one minute. Ask the children to freeze then tap individuals on the shoulder, inviting them to share their thoughts. Ask them how they feel and what they can see and hear.

Show examples of picture postcards from holiday destinations and explain to the class that they are going to send a picture postcard from the moon in role as a moon tourist. Give each child a blank postcard to illustrate, drawing on their experiences from the guided walk.

Session four:

Writing in role and shared writing

Share examples of the children's postcard illustrations and discuss what information the class might include on a postcard from the moon. Using shared writing compose the opening of an appropriate message with the children. You can also model the writing of the address, drawing attention to the specific layout, before asking the class to write their own postcards to someone they know such as a family member or friend.

Don't forget the moon stamps!

Session five:

Design and technology

Look again at the illustration of Bob's souvenir stall and ask the children in pairs to think of what else he could sell. Some examples might be moon mints in the shape of a crescent moon, moon music CDs for relaxation, space pens in the shape of a rocket, moon fact files and moon joke books.

Collect the ideas into the class journal and invite the children to sketch, label and price objects they think would make popular additions to the range.

Ask each child to choose one item to make for the stall. Organise the class into groups according to what they want to make. Provide a range of modelling materials and ensure that joke books are available for those who need them for support in writing their own.

When the objects are ready, make sure that they are appropriately labelled and priced ready for the souvenir stall which you have already set up in the reading or role play area.

Session six:

Shared writing and illustrating

In the story we hear that astronauts often create extra work for Bob by dropping litter. Explain that the class can help him by composing a list of instructions. Discuss what visitors to the moon should be aware of. For example, they should remember to take their litter home and make sure that they stay out of the craters when the red flags are flying; they should always put on their walking boots and space helmets before leaving the space ship, and remember to turn off all mobile phones as they interfere with the moon music.

Record the children's ideas on a double page of the class journal, leaving enough space around the edges of the text to add illustrations. Give the children a small piece of paper and ask them to illustrate one of the instructions. Cut out the illustrations and add them to the list.

Sessions seven and eight:

Art and design

In order to keep his job, Bob has to find a way of attracting more tourists to the moon. Explain that you are going to help him do this by designing a poster - A Day Trip to the Moon.

Drawing on what the class already know from the book, their own virtual experiences and from information books, ask groups to list features that would attract visitors. These might include attractions such as the creepy craters and moon music and the thrill of supersonic travel, the chance to make your own moon movies and try moon walking lessons, or the spectacle of Bob doing his somersaults.

In their groups, ask the children to design their own posters to attract more tourists to the moon.

Session nine:

Drama and role-play

Re-read the book, this time asking the class to spot all the aliens in the pictures. Ask the children in pairs to imagine that they are one of these aliens and to describe themselves: their names, ages, where they live (on earth or the moon), what they enjoy doing, whether they have any special powers and what they think of Bob and the tourist space ships. Get them to draw their alien and make a story prop or paper bag puppet. Ask these pairs to team up with another pair and, in role, introduce themselves, including as much relevant detail as they can.

Invite pairs to come the front of the class to be interviewed about their daily routines.

Sessions ten and eleven:

Drama and role-play, bookmaking

Tell the children that they are going to create a TV talk show interview. Agree on a title for the show and then allocate different roles such as the TV presenter, Bob, a tourist and a couple of aliens. The rest of the class become the studio audience.

If this is the first time they have done something like this, you might want to go into role as the TV presenter. Confident users of ICT can film the show while others can act as photographers and take digital photographs which can be made into an electronic book using photo story or printed as a paper version.

Sessions twelve, thirteen and fourteen:

Shared writing and writing in role

Explain to the class that they are going to write a sequel to *Man on the Moon: a day in the life of Bob.* It could be, for example, Aliens on the Moon? A day in the life of … give the children a large sheet of sugar paper and, in groups, ask them to sketch out the different parts of an alien's day: what they do every day, who they meet, how they hide from Bob, what time they go home, where they live. Draw on the children's ideas to create a shared writing account of a new story.

Using their notes, ask the children to write their individual accounts of their alien's day, starting each section with a new paragraph. When they are written, ask the children to work in pairs to read their finished draft to a partner. They can then revise and edit these, before going on to write and illustrate the final version in individual home-made books.

Session fifteen:

Information writing, researching space

Talk to the children about what they already know about space. Decide what they would like to know more about and put them into five groups to research an aspect that they are interested in. Provide a collection of relevant information books and resources and have useful website links ready on the desktop. Collate this information in a class Moon Fact File. This can be in paper or electronic form. When they are finished display them alongside the other information resources for children to read.

Grace and Family
Mary Hoffman and Caroline Binch
A teaching sequence of 2 to 3 weeks

Learning aims

- To discuss themes and issues that arise in this moving story, enabling children to make connections with their own lives

- To explore and develop ideas through talk and to respond to each other's responses

- To develop creative responses to the text through drama, play and drawing

- To write in role in order to explore characters and events

- To reflect on reading through the keeping of a reading journal

This is an engaging picture book which deals sensitively with the important experiences of family, difference, separation and reunion.

A sequel to *Amazing Grace,* this concerns Grace's feelings of difference from conventional family groups and her emotions and dilemmas when invited to visit her father and his new family in the Gambia. Accompanied by her wise Nana, Grace gradually learns to deal with her feelings of being an outsider to her Gambian family. Their warm welcome enables Grace to accept them and to enjoy being a loved member of two families.

As someone who enjoys stories, Grace begins hopeful of a happy ending, with her family reunited. But by the end she understands that the concept of 'family' can include different patterns and experiences.

Caroline Binch's illustrations are detailed and vivid, allowing children to explore the emotions and relationships they describe and the worlds they bring to life.

Key Teaching Approaches

Reading aloud and re-reading

Class reading journal

Booktalk

Writing in role

Drawing and annotating

Re-enactment through play

Visualising

Shared writing

Researching and information writing

> What we know already about Grace.
>
> She likes to play different roles in plays.
>
> She is a very confident girl.
>
> She likes to participate in acting in her class.
>
> Grace lives with her nan.
>
> She loves to listen to stories even if they were from her imaginations.
>
> She likes ballet.
>
> She lives with her dad, mum, nan and a cat.
>
> Amazing Grace
>
> She likes acting out stories even at home.
>
> She sticks her mind to what she wants to do.
> She never lets herself

Session one:

The class reading journal

Begin this unit of work on *Grace and Family* by reading aloud *Amazing Grace,* the first story of Grace, and inviting the children to discuss together what they already know about her. Then, using a large class reading journal, scribe children's ideas about Grace around an enlarged image of her on the first page.

Include what the children know about Grace's family such as who she lives with and which members of the family they have already met, and record these in the journal.

Session two:

Writing in role

Read the first two double spreads of *Grace and Family.* Show and then read aloud an extract that you have previously written in the class journal from 'Grace's diary' before she has received the invitation to Africa with comments such as, "Why can't I have a proper family?" "If only my father lived at home with us too."

As a class, share ideas about how Grace feels when she hears about her father's invitation to visit his family in The Gambia and note them down in the class journal. Then ask the children to write a diary entry, in role as Grace, expressing her thoughts and feelings about visiting her father. Children can be given, or make, little books to use as diaries throughout the sequence.

Session three:

Role-play

Read aloud the whole story.
Ask the children to work in groups of six or seven to create a freeze-frame of Grace and her Gambian family: father, stepmother, nana, sister, brother and dog. Allow time for groups to practise their scene before they present them to the class. 'Unfreeze' some of the children, asking them to voice their thoughts in role.

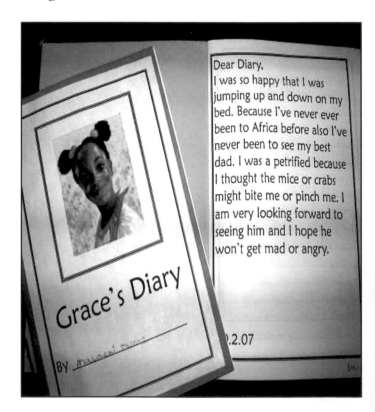

Grace's Diary
By _____

Dear Diary,
I was so happy that I was jumping up and down on my bed. Because I've never ever been to Africa before also I've never been to see my best dad. I was a petrified because I thought the mice or crabs might bite me or pinch me. I am very looking forward to seeing him and I hope he won't get mad or angry.

.2.07

Session four:

Drawing and annotating

Discuss with the class the notion of different kinds of families. Ask them to draw and annotate their own families and display these pictures. They can draw from memory or bring in photographs. Show some examples to help them choose different forms of display including illustrated family trees, a collection of miniature portraits or a family map. For variety, children can also be offered different materials to use to create their display such as pencil, pen or charcoal.

Session five:

Discussion and writing

Talk to the children about their pictures and Grace's statement that her family isn't right. What does Nana mean by *'families are what you make them?'*
Have a class circle time with a sentence to be finished with, *"A family is…"*
Afterwards, children can write down what their family means to them, what they like about their family and about particular family members giving examples both from nowadays and from family memories.

Sessions six and seven:

Writing in role

Make time for the children to write several entries in their diaries in role as Grace. They can choose to write about a few of the key points in the narrative. They might, for example, write about her arrival in the Gambia and her first day with her new family, her phone conversation with her mother or the visit to the food market. Other entries might focus on the farewell party, the crocodiles or how she felt about leaving Africa.

Suggest children use drawings to record what she did.

Session eight:

Visualising and painting

Ask the children to shut their eyes and try to visualise the Gambian market. Ask them to describe to a partner what they could see. Then share some of these ideas. Re-read the part of the book that focuses on the market. Ask children to say what they liked about the way this part is written and illustrated, and note down their comments in the class reading journal. Children can then paint different scenes of the market place.

Session nine:

Illustrating

Focus on the phrase 'stepping inside a rainbow' and talk with the children about what this means. Collect together a selection of African fabrics and discuss together the colours, patterns and motifs. The children should paint or print their own African designs on paper or fabric.

Session ten:

Re-enactment through play

With the children's help create an African market in the role-play area that is like 'stepping into a rainbow'. Provide fabrics for the children to wear, and baskets and other artefacts, and fruit and vegetables to buy. Make opportunities for reading and writing that there could be in a market such as labels, prices, shopping lists, advertising slogans and jingles. Make time for groups to take turns 'going to market'.

Session eleven:

Writing in role

Using shared writing and a flip chart write a post-card from Grace to her friends back in England, telling them about her best time in The Gambia. Children can then go on to write their own postcard in role. Children should illustrate the card too, with a scene from the places she visited.

Session twelve:

Researching The Gambia, information writing

Using a large world map or globe show children where they can find The Gambia.
Talk with the class about any personal connections they might have with African countries and plot these onto an enlarged map of the continent. Then go on to include other countries that children come from around the world onto a world map.

Make a display of books, artefacts, posters and other materials such as foods from Africa and suggest children use these to put together a fact file. More independent writers will enjoy writing their own information books about an aspect of African life that interests them.

Session thirteen:

Find out more about the author

Put together a display of other books by Mary Hoffman to share and talk about in read aloud times. Encourage the children to browse and share their favourites with others in independent or group reading times. Children can find out more about the author by looking together at Mary Hoffman's website: **www.maryhoffman.co.uk**

Lila and the Secret of Rain

David Conway & Jude Daly

A teaching sequence of 4 to 5 weeks

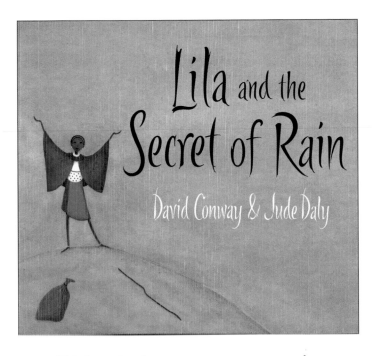

This is a tale of courage, perseverance and, above all, of hope that speaks to us of the vital relationship that exists between people and the natural world.

Lila's Kenyan village is suffering a terrible drought. It is so hot that no one can bear to be out in it. In the remorseless heat the crops and the cattle begin to die, and the wells to dry up. When Lila hears her mother say that "without water there can be no life" she is so worried that she sets out on a quest to uncover the secret of rain and so save the village.

This modern folk tale is a reminder of how necessary and precious water is for everyone's survival. It provides a starting point to explore larger themes of conservation and to consider ways in which individuals can make an active contribution. Jude Daly's beautiful, expressive illustrations create an unrelenting sun-blasted landscape within which the sparse simplicity of David Conway's quietly poetic text unfolds.

Learning aims

- To talk confidently about a book, exploring, developing and sustaining ideas through discussion

- To explore and interpret stories through creative activity, including drama, storytelling, music and art

- To use both fiction and non-fiction books to find out about and develop an understanding of another cultural and geographical setting

- To write a variety of chronological and non-chronological texts for real purposes and audience

Key Teaching Approaches

Booktalk

Responding to illustration

Re-enactment through play

Storymapping

Storytelling

Writing in role

Performance

Shared writing

Information writing

Bookmaking

Debate and argument

Before beginning this unit of work:

Collect together other stories set in Kenya as well as a range of information texts, posters, artefacts and photographic materials. Encourage both children and adults to draw on this collection during independent and supported reading times. Designate a specific time in the day for looking together as a class at a particular book or photograph from the collection and encourage children to talk about their own discoveries or enthusiasms as a regular part of the session.

Session one:

Responding to illustration

Begin by talking with the children about the weather. Ask them who likes sunny days best, and who likes it best when it rains.
Ask the children what they think would happen if the sun shone every day and it never rained.
How do they think they would feel then?
Some children may have personal experience of living in countries where they have experienced the more destructive aspects of the sun.

Show the children the first double page spread of the book with the text covered and ask them to talk together about it. You could either do this as a whole class using the interactive whiteboard or in groups using laminated copies.

As a class share these first responses and list any questions onto a flip chart to refer back to later.

Session two:

Booktalk

Revisit the first page of the book and ask the class how they think they would be feeling if they were one of the children in the village.
Share some of the children's ideas before going on to read aloud to the part where Lila leaves the village on her quest to tell the sky the saddest things she knows. Discuss with the children what sorts of things these might have been.
What do they think would be sad enough to make the sky cry?
Ask the children to imagine that they are Lila and to tell the person next to them what they would say.
As shared writing write one or two of the children's ideas into prepared speech bubbles.
Children can now work independently to write their own ideas into a speech bubble of their own and add them to the display.

Booktalk and storymapping

Read the book aloud from the beginning.
Using the 'Tell me' questions, talk with the
children about their reactions to the story. Focus
on those aspects that they found most interesting,
moving or surprising. Read some of these parts out
loud again for them to hear the original language.
What do they think this story is about?

Put the children into pairs with large sheets of
paper and ask them to draw a story map of the
story. Suggest they annotate it by adding two or
three speech bubbles and by including some of
their favourite phrases. Finally, they should write
a beginning and an end for their story. When the
maps are finished each pair should use them to
help retell the story to another pair of children.

Re-enactment through play

Begin to make a tabletop 3-dimensional
geographical map of the story using sand, dried
grass and a material such as mod-roc to make the
mountains. Provide materials such as pipe-cleaners
and material scraps for children to use to make the
villagers and the animals. When it is finished put
aside some regular time for children to use the
map for re-enacting the story and for making their
own tales.

Storytelling and role-play

Sit the children down in a large storytelling circle
to 'pass the story round' with occasional support
from you as narrator. As you do so pause occasionally and invite children to come into the middle of
the circle to act out significant parts from the story.

Hot seating

Invite children to go into role as different
characters from the story and to come up in turn
to take the 'hot seat' and answer the class's
questions about what happened, how they felt
and what they thought.

Writing in role

Ask children to write the story from the viewpoint
of one of the characters. They might, for example,
write in role as Lila herself, her grandfather or her
mother. Someone might even choose to tell the
story from the viewpoint of the sky!

Shared writing and painting the story

As a class, and with you acting as scribe, map out
the main events of the story and summarise each
of them with a title and a caption. Children paint
illustrative panels for each of the sections and
finally present the whole as a wall story.

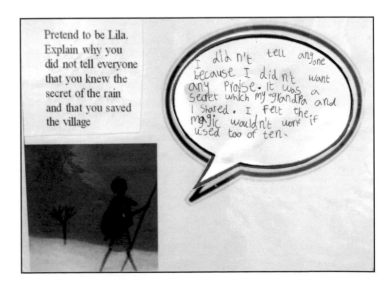

Pretend to be Lila. Explain why you did not tell everyone that you knew the secret of the rain and that you saved the village

I didn't tell anyone because I didn't want any praise. It was a secret which my grandpa and I shared. I felt the magic wouldn't work if used too often.

Song writing

When it finally starts to rain the whole village celebrates with music and dancing.
Using shared writing to help shape the children's ideas begin to write a song together to celebrate the coming of the rain, using the call and response pattern that characterises the singing of some Kenyan peoples. This will provide a strong supportive pattern for the children to work within. You might use the themes and imagery of the book as a starting point, for example:

A: *Thank you for the rain*
B: It feels like kisses on our cheeks

A: *Thank you for the rain*
B: It makes our crops grow tall and green
Children should go on to write their own songs using the same open framework. When these are finished collect the songs into a class song book or put them onto laminated song cards. Encourage children to draw on the patterns and colours of traditional Kenyan textile and art work for their illustrations.

Performing the song

When the class song is finished put the children into small groups to read it through together and prepare it for performance. Each group might be given the whole song to work with or a section of it. Ask the children to decide how they might choose to perform the song most effectively. For example, will they read all or some of it in unison, in parts or as individuals? Should some parts be whispered while others are shouted?
Once they have finished the class should go on to perform the song in an assembly or to another class.

Music and dance

Work together as a class to improvise a short piece of music to convey the coming of the storm. Each group of children could work with a different set of instruments, for example, chime bars or drums, or use body music such as clapping and clicking.

When finished record the piece and work with the children to create a dance to depict the villagers' response to the arrival of the rains.

Sessions sixteen and seventeen:

Finding out about Kenya

Ask the children what they think it would be like to grow up in Kenya.
Do they think all of Kenya is like the country depicted in this book?

Show the children where Kenya is on the world map using a large world map or the interactive whiteboard. Tell them that as this book portrays life in only one part of the vast country that is Kenya they are going to do some research to find out some things about what it would be like to be a child living in different parts of Kenya and compare what life is like in the country with life in the town.

First, browse the internet together to find out answers to some of the children's first questions such as what is the capital city of Kenya or how many people live in Kenya. Show the class how to look for photographic images and browse some together.

Talk with the children about the sorts of things they would like to find out about and mind map their suggestions gathering linked ideas together under categories such as food, clothes, houses… (It might be useful to refer back to the list of questions that came out of the picture activity when discussing these.)

Prepare a large poster-size comparison chart.

Children will use this to help them sort information as they work.

Put the children into small groups to research specific questions working with a variety of information texts as well as internet sources. As they work, suggest children write each relevant

Session fifteen:

Visualising and painting

Listen to some traditional West African music such as that of traditional kora musicians N'Faly & Dunyakan Kouyate.
Talk with the children about the sorts of pictures that it creates in their mind's eye as they listen.
Replay the music and listen again.
What is it about the way that the music is played that creates these pictures for the listener?
Children go on to paint these pictures either as the music plays or when it has finished.

For example, they might want to know:

	Country areas	Town and cities
What do children eat?		
What do the children do?		
Where do children live?		
What do children wear?		

fact that they discover onto a post-it note, and stick these into the appropriate sections of the chart. The information on these post-its can then be discussed, elaborated on or discarded when the group comes to write up the findings from their research.

Confident writers can go on to work on their own or in pairs.

Less confident writers can be supported through-out this work in guided writing, first reading and talking together about a page or two of information text with an adult, and then writing notes together. They could then go on to write independently.

Jamie remembered his mother telling him about a magical instrument which his great, great grandfather used to play. It was a flute.

Sessions eighteen and nineteen:

Information writing

Ask the children to write and illustrate a non-fiction text using the information that has been collected. This could be done in a variety of ways, for example, they might write tourist leaflets about Kenya, make an annotated map or work as individuals or together as a group to make an information book.

Session twenty:

Debate and discussion

Lila's mother says that "without water there can be no life" so Lila is afraid that the village will not survive the drought.
Talk with the children about whether they think water is an equally precious thing here in England. Should we be more careful how we use it? Discuss with the class the sorts of things that could be done both within society as well as individuals to conserve water.

Children go on to design and draw posters to encourage others to use water wisely.

Mufaro's Beautiful Daughters

John Steptoe

A teaching sequence of 2 to 3 weeks

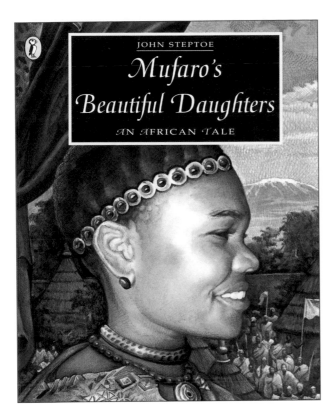

Learning aims

- To discuss the themes and morals of the story, enabling children to make connections with their own lives

- To explore, sustain and develop ideas through talk and to listen to each other's responses

- To develop creative responses to the text through drama, role-play, drawing and writing

- To reflect on reading, to explore characters and events through keeping a reading journal

- To engage children with a traditional story to develop their understanding of the genre and the cross-cultural, cross-time nature of story

This tale, based on a Zimbabwean traditional Cinderella story, is memorably told and beautifully illustrated. It tells the story of two sisters who respond very differently to an invitation to meet the King who is searching for a wife. The pattern of events the sisters encounter on their journey to the palace from their village home reveal their true individual natures and determine who will be Queen. The detailed illustrations provide rich contexts for talk and the story offers children opportunities to explore moral values and concepts of beauty, and to make connections with Cinderella stories from different cultures.

Key Teaching Approaches

Responding to illustration

The class journal

Booktalk

Storymapping

Storytelling

Re-enactment through play

Comparison grid

Drama and role-play

Writing in role

Research and information reading

Responding to illustration and the class reading journal

As a way of introducing the book, but before reading the story to the children, show the whole book cover, the front and back covers side by side, perhaps using an interactive whiteboard.
Ask the children to think about what they think they know about the girls from looking at the cover illustration and what specific evidence they are drawing on. You can scribe their comments in a class journal around the illustrations of both sisters, one on each page.

Reading aloud and booktalk

Show the cover again and ask children to predict what they think the story will be about and what kind of story it might be. Ask them to share their reasons. Scribe their ideas on a new page of the journal.

Then read the story aloud pausing to share the illustrations as you read.
Talk with the class about their responses to the story: their likes and dislikes, particularly focusing on any questions they have and the things that the story reminds them of. Write their responses in the class journal using the 'Tell me' headings. Children might also work in groups writing their responses onto post-its and place them in the class journal.

Storymapping

Re-read the story aloud. As a class, ask the children to remember the key points in the story and list these on a flip chart. Go on to sketch a map of the beginning of the story and involve the children in building a visual sequence of events. Then, in twos or threes, using large sheets of paper, children can map the whole story and annotate their drawings with speech or thought bubbles, or phrases remembered from the story.

Storytelling

Using their storymaps to help them, children can practise retelling the story by 'passing the story on' in their group. They can join up with another group, with each taking a turn to tell their story. Then, as a whole group, ask the children to reflect on what they learned about storytelling. What helped them to tell the story? What happens to the story with each retelling?

Book-based game

Collect together some simple board games and materials for making a game including card, glue, scissors, pens, large squared paper, counters and dice.

Begin by asking the whole class to think about the board games they already know. Use a selection of the games they mention and other simple games to introduce the activity and provide children with different models such as snakes and ladders and a track or storymap game with a start and finish (see also CLPE's *Book-based Reading Games* for more ideas). What elements of the storyworld and characters can they include in their game? It will be helpful to sketch out some ideas on a flip chart with the children's help, before dividing them into groups to devise their own games.

In groups of three or four, children should collaborate to design and make a game based on the story. They can plan their game first and then gather the materials they need.

When complete they can play the game to test it and then show other groups how to play it, writing instructions to go with their game.

Comparison grid

Create a display of different versions of the Cinderella story. There are many examples to draw on such as *Wishbones: A Folk Tale from China* by Barbera Ker Wilson, *The Little Blue Slipper, An Irish Cinderella Story* by Jude Daly. Choose one from the collection to introduce and read it aloud.
In what ways is this story similar to *Mufaro's Beautiful Daughters*? What differences do they notice?

Record the children's ideas as a comparison chart into the class journal.
In groups children can work in a similar way to discuss and analyse the similarities and differences of the other Cinderella stories. When they are finished bring the class together for a final class discussion.

Role-play and writing in role

In pairs, children can each take the role of one sister.

What would they say to each other when no-one else is listening? Why is Manyara so proud and selfish?
Still in pairs, children can perform their conversation/argument to another group and some might like to present theirs to the whole class.

While still in role, children write about one sequence of events as a diary entry.

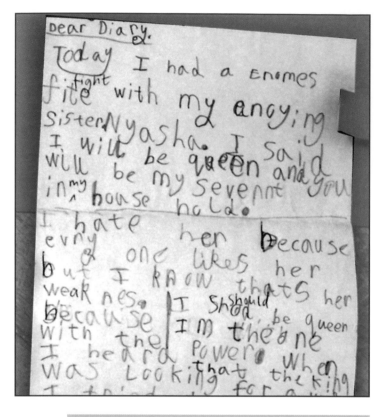

Dear Diary.
Today I had a Enemes fite (fight) with my anoying sister Nyasha. I said I will be queen and you will be my sevant in my house hald. I hate evry one her because but I know thats her weak nes. I should I be queen because I'm the one I heard power when I was looking for the king

Session nine:

Hot seating

What does Mufaro think and feel about his daughters? How did they become so different? How will life change for him after the wedding? And what happens as they all grow older?

These are some of the questions the children might like to ask him. What other questions would they also like answers to? They can ask questions as a character in the story, for example: a villager, a daughter, the girls' mother, the King or one of his courtiers or servants. In pairs, ask the children to think together and write a list of some of their questions.

Ask for a volunteer or choose one child to take on the role of Mufaro and ask the rest of the class to hot seat him.

Session ten:

Research and information reading

On a globe or world map, help the children to locate Africa and the country of Zimbabwe, and if possible the city of Nyanda, the walled city of Great Zimbabwe, where the story takes place. This was a main trading centre of the Shona people where they sold gold, copper and ivory to Arab merchants.

What do children already know about Zimbabwe? What do they want to find out? Record these responses in the journal alongside a map of the country.

Make and display a themed collection of information books and other storybooks about Zimbabwe, past and present, and share images and further information using the interactive whiteboard.

Mia's Story
A Sketchbook of Hopes and Dreams
Michael Foreman

A teaching sequence of 3 to 4 weeks

Learning aims

- To discuss issues raised by the story and readers' responses to characters and events

- To explore and interpret stories through creative activity

- To develop an understanding of another cultural and geographical setting through the use of both fiction and non-fiction texts

- To write about thoughts and feelings through writing in role and writing poetry

Key Teaching Approaches

Booktalk

Word collections

Storymapping

Drawing and annotating

Drama and role-play

Bookmaking

Writing in role

Information writing

Shared writing

This is a powerful and touching story of human resourcefulness, spirit and hope against the odds. It was inspired by the story of a family that Michael Foreman met living on a dump in the Andes.

Mia lives with her family in a small South American village beneath the snowy mountains of the Andes. They make their living by reclaiming and recycling the dumped junk of the city. In this way the family dream of one day being able to replace their shanty home with one built of bricks. One day, Mia's father brings home a puppy which she calls Poco because he's so small. When Poco goes missing, Mia travels far up into the mountains to search for him. There she finds some beautiful white mountain flowers which she brings home. Soon these flowers are flourishing so well in their new home that Mia and her father have a new product to sell, one that is so in demand that they can hope to realise their dream.

Michael Foreman tells the story through a clever combination of intimate drawings with hand-written captions and large landscape watercolours.

Before beginning this unit of work:

Put together a collection of Michael Foreman's books. Read aloud regularly from this collection at story times and set time aside in which children can revisit these books for themselves in shared and independent reading times.

What do the children like about the way in which Michael Foreman paints and draws?

It will be important to provide frequent opportunity throughout this sequence of work for children to experiment with pencil, watercolour and soft papers to see if they can paint in the style of Michael Foreman.

Session one:

Booktalk and reading aloud

Introduce the book by showing the children the picture of Mia on the front cover at the same time as you read the blurb on the back to them.
Can they imagine what living on a rubbish dump would be like?

Show the children the endpapers where the village is approached across the sprawl of the rubbish dump.
Talk with them about their first responses, making a note of any questions and comments that they have.

Read the book aloud to the end. Using the 'Tell me' questions discuss with the children the things they like or don't like about the story. Talk with them about their first responses to the illustrations. Return to look closely at the ones that children are particularly struck by.
Why do they think the book is called 'a sketchbook of hopes and dreams'?

Capture the discussion using a flip chart, the notepad on the interactive whiteboard or as part of a class journal for referring back to later.

Session two:

Word collections

Read the story again. Is there anything about the ways in which Michael Foreman has used language in the story that the children particularly notice? Make a list of any words or phrases that children recall as you talk about them together and pin them up as a wordbank for children to use in their own writing. This list can be added to as children work with the sequence.

Session three:

Drawing and annotating

What do the children think Mia is like?
Ask them to work in pairs to draw an outline of Mia. Around the outside of the outline they should write everything they know about her from reading the book and inside the outline they write what they think they know about her as a person.

My Lost Doll By Amira

I loved my dollie
I brought it
every where.

good night

one day I
went to my cousin's
house. we played
dollies. It was bed
time and we put
are dollies away.

Mapping the story

Make a 3D map of the village and the surrounding mountains. Provide a variety of collage materials and encourage children to draw on the illustrations and the text of the book in deciding the detail.

Role-play

Re-read the book from the point at which Mia's father brings Poco home to the part where Poco goes missing.

How do the children think Mia is feeling?

Ask them to go into role as Mia and to first act out and then freeze-frame the moment when she realises Poco is lost.
Go round the groups in turn and ask the children to tell you how they are feeling.
Make a list to return to later.

Storytelling and bookmaking

Remind children of the list of feelings that they compiled previously before asking them:

Has anything like this ever happened to you?

Put children into pairs to tell each other their stories before giving them folded paper books in which to draw and write their own stories. Less experienced writers could write a shared story in guided writing.

Session seven:

Drawing and annotating

Children work in pairs or as individuals to draw an annotated map of the search for Poco and adding speech bubbles.

Session eight:

Writing and performing poetry

Re-read the part where Mia climbs above the city into the shining white snow of the snow-capped mountain. Ask the children to think and talk together about any personal memories of snow that they have.

Do they think snow is special? What makes it special?

Show them a short collection of photographic images of snow-covered mountains. And ask them to talk together about what they can see and how the images make them feel.
Put the children into groups and give each one of them a strip of card. Ask each group member to write a line to express something about their

response. All of the group's contributions can now be arranged between them to make a poem. Suggest the group consider whether they want to repeat any of the lines for effect.

Each group should now prepare their poem for performance deciding which lines should, for example, be spoken in unison or said as singular voices, shouted or whispered, before going on to perform it for an audience.

Sessions nine, ten and eleven:

Hot seating and writing in role

Ask the children who they think is telling this story. How do they know? Do they think somebody else from the village would tell the story differently?

Invite different characters in turn to come and talk with the class about what happens to Mia. Children go on to write Mia's story from the viewpoint of one of the characters. They might, for example, write in role as Mia herself, her father or her mother.

When they have finished children can present their work in a variety of ways. They could choose to write and illustrate a book, to make an electronic version using powerpoint, or even to compile a video diary.

Researching and information writing

Show the children where Chile is on the world map using a large map or the interactive white-board. Tell them that they are going to do some research to find out some more things about what the country of Chile is like and compare what life is like there with life in England.

Put together a powerpoint of photographic images of Chile and suggest the children talk in pairs about the ones that they find most interesting. You might include a sound file of pan pipes playing to accompany it. Discuss this display as a class and revisit some of the images together. Make a list of the things that interest the children most and that they want to find out more about.

Put children into groups with the same interests to find out what they can about their chosen area and to present their finished research as a large poster.

Drawing

Remind children of the first discussion they had about the 'sketchbook of hopes and dreams' and what it might contain.
What are their thoughts now?
What would they put in a sketchbook such as this?

Talk together as a class about their ideas before giving each child a small piece of quality white paper or card and materials and asking them to draw something that they or their family are hoping for or dreaming about. Invite children to talk to the class about what they have chosen.

Shared writing

Provide the class with an open beginning sentence such as 'These are my hopes and dreams, I dream of...' and write a list poem together. Read through the poem together and discuss how adding or altering the choice of a word or a phrase can change the effect. Are there lines that they would like to repeat?

Children go on to work pairs to write their own poems before performing them to each other, to another class or for an assembly.

The Puffin Book of Fantastic First Poems

June Crebbin (editor)

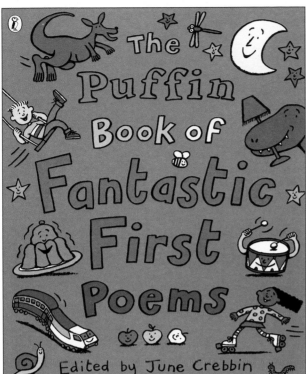

A teaching sequence of 2 to 3 weeks

Learning aims

- To hear, read and enjoy a range of poetry

- To talk confidently about individual responses to a poem

- To respond to poems through discussion, performance and illustration

- To recognise how poets select words and use patterns of rhythm, rhyme and sound to create effects

- To compose own poems

This vibrant anthology is a treasure trove of contemporary and traditional poems offering the readers lots of opportunity to have fun with language. It builds successfully on experience of traditional rhyme by introducing a wide range of poetry written by some of our finest poets. These poems are ideal for committing to memory, for performance and choral reading. Beautifully illustrated throughout, the collection is well laid out in popular categories with which children can readily engage. The categories also fit in well with a topic based curriculum.

This unit of work provides children with an opportunity to hear, read and respond to a selection of poems, thereby enhancing their enjoyment of language and encouraging them to experiment with new vocabulary and ideas in their own poetry writing.

Key Teaching Approaches

Poetry talk

Performing poetry

Visualising

Shared writing

Poetry writing

Before beginning this unit of work:

Create a poetry friendly environment by displaying a range of poetry books and examples of the class's favourite poems and rhymes. Remember to include poetry recordings in your listening area. You can provide sticky notes on which the children can write a comment to attach to a particular poem in a book. Encourage and build in opportunities for the children to browse, discuss and respond to the poems. You should aim to include a poetry performance or a read aloud time every day, drawing on these poems and others that the children collect or generate themselves. You might also like to introduce skipping rhymes for the children to enjoy in the playground and collect any playground rhymes they already know.

Poems are written to be heard in the first instance and it is therefore crucial that each poem should first be read aloud to the class or group, before displaying the text.

The focus of initial ideas for working with *The Puffin Book of Fantastic First Poems* is on poems with a food theme. However, these approaches can be used to explore the other themes in the book in a similar way.

Prepare a large class journal in which to record the children's observations and responses to the poems.

Session one:

Poetry talk
Spaghetti

Before reading the poem aloud to the class, make the experience more memorable by starting with a plate of real spaghetti. Allow the children to taste and smell it and discuss the texture, before recording in the class journal the descriptive words and phrases or questions which this generates. Say the word 'spaghetti' together, discussing the sound of it, drawing attention to its Italian roots, identifying the syllables and experimenting with different ways of saying it.

Session two:

Poetry talk

Without displaying the text, read the poem aloud to the class, asking the children to close their eyes and listen out for any words or lines they particularly like. Discuss briefly in pairs and take feedback. Re-read the poem, again without displaying it, and ask the children to listen for these and any other memorable words and lines.

Take feedback as before. Are there any parts they heard this time which they hadn't notice the first time? Have they changed their initial responses?

Using the interactive whiteboard, display the poem and highlight the particular words and phrases that the children identified whilst listening. What do they notice about these words? What makes these words memorable? Is it the way they sound, the images they evoke or simply that they are new to them? Discuss which words they would emphasise to heighten the listeners' enjoyment if they were to read the poem aloud.

In mixed groups of six, give the children individual copies of the poem. Allow plenty of time to practise taking it in turns to read the poem aloud round the group and to decide which words and phrases the children want to emphasise to make the most impact.

Invite each group to perform their version of the poem with the rest of the class giving feedback on the performance and interpretation.

Session three:

'Tell me' and choral reading

Without displaying the text, read aloud *Sounds Good,* inviting the class to listen out for words or lines that they particularly like. Ask the children to discuss their initial responses with a partner. After sharing these with the whole class, display the text for the first time and read it aloud together. Use the 'Tell me' questions to discuss the poem. Highlight the parts which the children find memorable and together read the poem aloud once more, savouring the sounds of the identified words and phrases. Divide up the three verses of the poem between the groups in preparation for a whole class choral reading. After giving the children time to practise, bring the three parts together as a class and present as a whole class choral reading, perhaps in assembly.

Session four:

Poetry talk and class performance

Read aloud *Dinosaur Dinner.* Discuss with the class which part they particularly liked and if it reminds them of anything. After sharing their responses, put the class into five groups and give each group two different verses stuck into the middle of an A3 sheet. Ask them to read their part of the poem aloud around the group a couple of times before choosing an aspect to illustrate, either individually or in pairs. They can then cut out the illustrations and stick them in the margins around the text. These pages will form the first part of a class anthology which will be added to as the unit progresses.

In sequence, invite the groups to read aloud their particular verses to the whole class, displaying their illustrations and saying why they chose them.

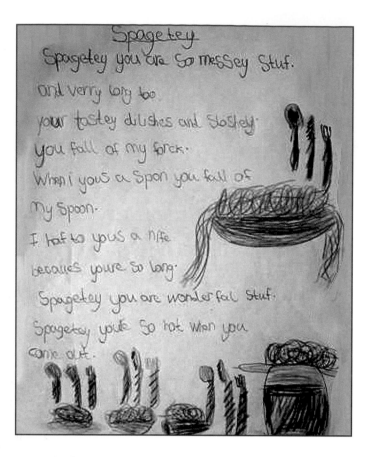

Poetry performance

Select five short poems from the anthology: for example, these could be *The Pancake, Breakfast, Toaster Time, Porridge Bubbling, Soggy Greens.*

Give an enlarged version of one poem to each group, without the illustrations, asking children to first read aloud their poem round the group and then to illustrate it. When they have completed their group illustrations, give each child an individual copy of the poem. Ask the group to prepare their poem for performance. They need to think about who will read each part, which parts will be read in unison, be repeated, shouted or whispered. Give the children plenty of time to rehearse their performance before presenting it to another class or for an assembly.

Shared writing and planning a poem

Read aloud two or three other food poems. Give the children time to discuss each one and record their responses in the class journal. Ask the children to think about their own favourite foods and to share any words and phrases which describe the way it looks, sounds, tastes, smells, the sensation of eating it, where and with whom they eat it. Take feedback and chose one of the foods suggested to model the planning of a class poem.

Draw the food in the middle of the page and record the children's contributions in the form of a thought shower to demonstrate how we can collect initial ideas to develop into a poem. Ask the children to work in pairs to record ideas about their own food in a similar way. Pairs can now share their plans with each other before sharing them with the whole class and inviting responses.

Shared writing

Chose one of the thought showers and discuss with the class which of the words, phrases or ideas they think would make a good opening line. With the children's help, begin to sequence the ideas, constantly re-reading and encouraging them to listen out for the way particular words and phrases sound as you do so. Are there any ideas which go together? Are there words or phrases they would like to use as a refrain? Model the redrafting process in the light of their comments.

Using their own thought showers, ask the pairs of children to begin to draft their own poems. Emphasise that, although most of the poems you have shared so far rhyme, not all poems have to rhyme and that sometimes including a rhyme just for the sake of it can spoil a poem.

Sessions nine and ten:

Redrafting and publishing the poems

Once the children have finished their first draft, use one pair's example to illustrate for the class the decisions that everyone needs to make in order to redraft and refine their poems. First read the example aloud and ask the children to

consider how it sounds and to decide if there are words or ideas they wish to omit or ones that they wish to add. Are they happy with the sequence of lines?

Children can now go on to work with a partner to revise their own drafts. Less confident writers will benefit from extra support.

After they have finished their final drafts, show the children how to edit their own work by reading one poem aloud to the class and asking them to comment on punctuation and spelling. They should now work with a partner to check and edit their own work before illustrating it ready for publication in the class anthology.

The Princess and the White Bear King
Tanya Robyn Batt

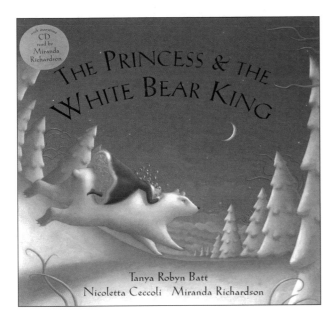

A teaching sequence of 4 to 5 weeks

Learning aims

- To talk confidently about picture books and responses individual to them

- To explore important themes of courage, perseverance and compassion

- To explore the story through a variety of teaching approaches including drama and role-play

- To write in role from more than one perspective

This longer more demanding book is a stirring story of betrayal, showing how love can be reclaimed through perseverance, endurance and compassion. Drawing on a combination of three folk tales from Northern Europe, this beautiful and complex picture book tells a dark adventure story that explores some powerful ideas and themes.
Far away in the distant north, a beautiful princess has a strange encounter with a great white bear who takes her to live in his castle. When she fails to pay attention to a warning and breaks a promise she has made, disaster strikes. The princess then sets out on an impossible journey which takes her east of the sun and west of the moon in the hope that she might redeem herself and break the spell.
This book is illuminated with enchanting pictures by award-winning illustrator Nicoletta Ceccoli which create the wintry landscape of this northern tale.

Key Teaching Approaches

Storytelling

Responding to illustration

Visualising

Drama and role-play

Drawing and annotating

Conscience alley

Mapping

Debate and argument

Writing in role

Bookmaking

Before beginning this story:

The Princess and the White Bear King is a very visual story and you will want to provide a variety of ways for children to conceptualise the world that it takes place in. Make some space on the classroom walls so that the princess's journey can be tracked across them as you work with the book.

You may also find it useful to give the children their own 'storyteller's journal'. This will help you to unfurl the story with the children and to sustain their reading. Put together a collection of folk tales which includes both picture and longer novel versions of the stories for children to explore and enjoy in both independent and guided reading sessions as well as for drawing on as a class read aloud.

Session one:

Storytelling

Prepare a storytelling bag with a selection of artefacts such as a small bell, a candle, a knife, a small tablecloth, a pair of 'silver' scissors, a golden cup, and a child-sized golden crown. Open it with the children and invite them to speculate with you as to what sort of story they might tell with the contents such as these. Invite children to help you to begin to make up a story or encourage them to make up their own stories using some of the artefacts as inspiration.

If children are not used to taking part in storytelling sessions like this it will be important to first give them some experience by working with a familiar story such as *Goldilocks and the Three Bears.*

Introduce children to the storytelling journals which they will work with as you read the book together.

Session two:

Responding to illustration

Show children the picture of the princess in bed on the interactive whiteboard and invite them to talk in pairs about their first responses to it. What sorts of comments/questions/observations do they have?
Share ideas as a class and write them around the edges of the picture for returning to later.

Session three:

Visualising

Read aloud to the bottom of the opening page in which the children hear about the princess's dream when she dreams of a crown that is 'brighter than the sun itself', and tell them that they are to be like the goldsmiths and make crowns of their own.

When the crowns are finished, set them out as a gallery for everyone to look at and appreciate. Suggest children talk about what they like about each other's work encouraging them to use the language of the story. Ask children to choose a crown to comment on and display it alongside the crown.
Children go on to photograph or draw their crown and place the picture in the journal with the comments alongside.

Role-play

Read aloud from "One day…" until "Then you are the one," purred the bear.

Ask pairs of children to role-play the conversation that happens between the princess and her father when she returns to the palace after walking in the forest and meeting the bear. Use the crowns to help set the scene.
In their journals children go on to write in role as the princess or the king writing their diary that night.

'Tell me' and word collections

Ask children to write an individual response to the story so far in their storytelling journal before using the 'Tell me' questions as a class to discuss together.
What do they like or not like about the story so far? Are there things that puzzle them? Talk with the class about the ways in which the author has used language to help the reader visualise the world of the story and begin to put together a collection of memorable words. Pin these up as part of the display.

Drawing and annotating

Discuss with the class what they think the princess is like.

What makes them think this? Do they like her? Children go on to draw a picture and add detailed annotations in their journals.

Mapping

Tell the children they are going to create a map of the first part of the story up to the point where the bear and the princess arrive at the castle. Then re-read the story aloud. Ask the children to make a geographical map, working in pairs on large sheets of paper with pastels and crayon to show what the land was like that lay between the palace and the bear's castle. When they have finished, children should label and annotate their maps and use these to help them write directions to help a visitor from home find their way.

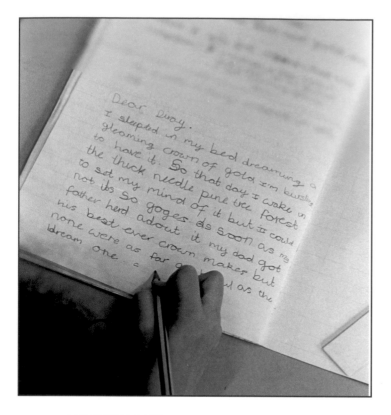

Discuss with the children what they think the princess should have done. Do they think she should have listened to her mother or should she have listened to the bear? Talk with the children about what the arguments are for taking one view or the other noting these down as a comparison chart.

Put the class into two groups. One group is to take the part of the mother's voice arguing for the princess to break her promise while the other group reminds her of all the reasons why she should keep it.

Go into role as teacher-in-role and walk between them. Which group is the most convincing?

Talk with the class about what they think will happen next in the story. What evidence do they have for thinking this? Ask them to draw their predictions as if they are the next three scenes of a film before going on to read aloud as far as the point where "she fell exhausted onto the forest floor."

They can use their storyteller's journal for this.

Ask children in pairs to share their predictions. How accurate were these? To what extent did they all agree?

Session eight:

Drawing and writing in role

Read aloud the description of the castle and ask children to imagine that they are the princess walking through its doors. What can they see? Make a gate-folded castle book out of a folded sheet of A4 and ask children to draw and annotate the inside of the castle within it.
Children go on to write another diary entry in role as the princess or the king describing their response to the day's events.

Session nine:

Conscience alley and drawing

Read aloud from "The princess explored the castle…" until the point where she returns to the castle and lies when the bear asks her if she has listened to her mother's advice.

Session ten:

Mapping 2

Read aloud the princess's journey to the point where she reaches the bottom of the glass mountain. Children can paint a second map to show what happens in this part of the story and map in detail the geographical setting.

Text marking

Read aloud the description of the princess's climb up the glass mountain.
Talk with the class about how the reader knows that this is a hard and difficult thing to do.
Use the interactive whiteboard to highlight the significant words together.
Ask children to go into role as the princess to show us what the climb would have been like.
Children go on to write another diary entry in role as the princess.

Debate and argument

Read aloud to the end of the third night when the prince and princess are reunited. The princess says that her gifts are "not for sale for gold or money". Ask the children what they think this means? What do they have that is not for sale for gold or money? Talk with the children about the things they have that are most precious to them and ask them to write what it is about them that puts them beyond price. When they have finished children should write their work out in their best handwriting, illustrate it and display it. A copy could be placed in their storyteller's journal.

Drama and role-play; writing in role

Put the children into twos. One is to imagine they are the kindly servant who looks after the prince while the other is to be the prince himself. Ask the children to role-play the conversation that might have happened between the two characters after the princess had visited for the second night. Children can work in pairs to write down the conversation.

Session fourteen:

Booktalk and discussion

How do the children think the story will end?
Put children into small groups to discuss their ideas for the ending before collecting together the class's ideas as a mind-map. Encourage each group to explain their reasons with reference to plot, character and genre.

Session fifteen:

Drama and role-play

Read aloud to the end of the story.
Put the class into groups to re-enact the final scene by the river. Children should take turns to go into role as the prince or the princess or the troll queen, or to be one of the wedding party. Give each group time to practise before sharing each group's work with the others in turn. Ask the audience to give feedback as to what they felt each group did that was particularly effective. Children can also video some of the action and play it back on the interactive whiteboard for admiration and comment. In what ways could the group improve or develop their work?

Session sixteen:

Hot seating

Discuss the character of the troll queen with the class. How do the children think the troll queen might have felt about what happens? Do they feel that the way the story ends is fair to her?
What questions would they like to ask her?
Invite the troll queen along for an interview.

Children go on to write in role as the troll queen in their storytelling journals

Sessions seventeen, eighteen and nineteen:

Bookmaking 1

With the class, and using shared writing, plot out the main events of the story and reorganise them into chronological order. Re-sort these so that they fit into no more than ten main sections. As a class, think of a chapter heading to fit each of these sections and decide where each chapter will begin and where it will end.

Children go on to work independently or in pairs to write a given part of the story in draft. As they work, ask them to stop occasionally to read parts of what they have written to a response partner. Ask them if there is anything they want to change - a section, sentences or phrases. When a whole section is complete it can be edited with the help of an editing partner.

Session twenty:

Bookmaking 2

Once each section is finished children can write a final copy of their story and illustrate it. The chapters can then be bound together to make complete books which can be placed in the book corner for everybody to enjoy.

A Fistful of Pearls

and other tales from Iraq

Elizabeth Laird

The nine stories in this folk story collection are re-told in a lively and humorous way. They tell the tales of boastful tailors, lazy husbands and clever hares set in a country that, today, is known to children for scenes of war and its aftermath on the television news.

Set in times long past, these stories have echoes of other familiar traditional tales but retain their individual cultural flavour when told by the author who has lived in Iraq. They provide opportunities for storytelling, discussing underlying meanings and visual interpretation. This teaching sequence encourages children to make connections between these tales and the traditional tales they know well.

A teaching sequence of 3 to 4 weeks

Learning aims

- To introduce children to some of the traditional stories of Iraq

- To enable children to engage in retelling and storytelling

- To make connections between traditional stories

- To explore story through a range of creative responses including drama, puppetry and art

- To write with confidence for real purposes and audiences

Key Teaching Approaches

Reading aloud and re-reading

Booktalk

Drama and role-play

Visualising

Storymapping

Performance

Bookmaking

Visualising

Read aloud the introduction to the book and ask the children to listen with their eyes closed and to create a 'film in their minds' from the descriptions. Working in pairs children should choose a scene from the introduction to illustrate using pencils and watercolours, perhaps adding annotation. As a class, find Iraq on a world map or globe and then look together at an enlarged map of Iraq. Children's drawings can be displayed around the large wall map and linked with corresponding places and areas of Iraq.

Lazy Ahmed

Booktalk

Read the story aloud and talk briefly with the children about their initial responses to it. Ask them what questions it raises for them and what other stories or experiences it reminds them of. What did they think the story was about? What underlying meanings do they think it holds? Give the children time to talk in pairs about the story before coming back together as a class to talk in more detail. Record their responses using a 'Tell me' grid on a flip chart.
Did talking together and hearing other children's ideas make them think about the story differently?

Storytelling

Re-read the beginning of the story and ask the class to recall key parts of the story. Note their ideas down as a list and together 'boil it down' into a sequence of four main events. Then, working in groups of four, and using this list as a prompt, the children move on to share the

retelling of the story, taking it in turns to tell one event each, in as much detail as they can, before passing the story on.

Working with A4 sheets of paper ask the children to write and illustrate their own part of the story. What sort of title might they give it? When these are finished they can be made into group books, read aloud to other groups for their comment and displayed in the book area for all to enjoy.

Zirak and the ring-dove

Storytelling with puppets

Read the story aloud and ask the children to share their ideas of what they think it is about.
List the characters on a flip chart (these include 1 ring dove, 3 grumpy sister doves, Zirak the rat and the birdcatcher) adding the children's descriptions of the characters. Encourage them to list both their physical characteristics and their obvious personality traits.

Working in groups of six, ask the children to each make a stick puppet of one of the characters to use in retelling the story, using a range of materials such as card, sticks, tissue paper, glue, pens or paint. They should spend some time practising their retelling of the story before performing to another group or to the whole class, using movement and sound effects.

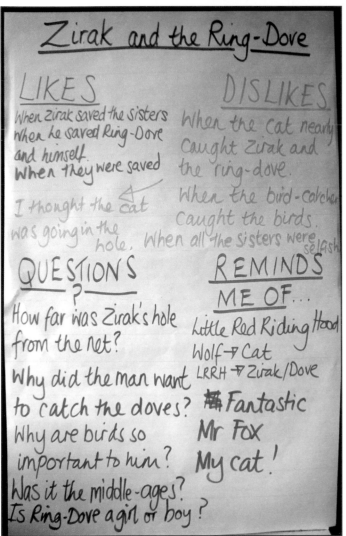

Zirak and the Ring-Dove

LIKES
When Zirak saved the sisters
When he saved Ring-Dove
and himself.
When they were saved

I thought the cat
was going in the
hole.

DISLIKES
When the cat nearly
caught Zirak and
the ring-dove.

When the bird-catcher
caught the birds.
When all the sisters were selfish

QUESTIONS ?
How far was Zirak's hole
from the net?

Why did the man want
to catch the doves?
Why are birds so
important to him?
Was it the middle-ages?
Is Ring-Dove a girl or boy?

REMINDS ME OF...
Little Red Riding Hood
Wolf → Cat
LRRH → Zirak/Dove

Fantastic
Mr Fox
My cat!

The moon pool

Role-play

Read the story aloud to the class before talking about it together, sharing likes and dislikes and focussing on anything that has puzzles them. What did they think about the elephants need for water? Were the hares right to keep it for themselves?

Ask the children to work in pairs in role as Firuz the Hare and the Elephant King. Ask them to role-play the conversation between the two animals with one child as Firuz the Hare, giving reasons for the hares needing to keep the elephants out of their territory and the other child being the Elephant King explaining why the elephants need to search for and take water. Do the class think it's possible to reach a compromise?

Invite some pairs to present their conversation to the rest of the class.
Then, on separate sheets of paper, children should draw their characters facing one another using speech bubbles to present their arguments. This can be very effective when shown as a vertical sequence, or zig-zag, of speech bubbles to give a flavour of the dialogue and the developing argument.

A fistful of pearls

Sessions eight and nine:

Storymapping

Read the story aloud.
Does this story remind them of any other stories they know? What elements do they have in common?

Ask the children to work in pairs to identify the six main events before going on to agree a final list as a class. Referring to these begin to draw a storymap with the children's help using simple sketches and annotation.

Working in groups of four, children go on to make their own storymap, adding illustrations and annotations.

Using their maps, groups retell the story, passing it around the group. They may decide to add more detail to their story map.

Sign of the tassel

Sessions ten and eleven:

Shared writing

Read the story aloud and talk with the children about their first responses.
What makes them angry? How do they feel when they are angry?

Using shared writing list their ideas and experiences.
What helps them to snap out of it and cheer up?

Working with writing partners the children should tell, and then write, about a time that they were angry, outlining what led up to it, how they reacted and what happened. As they work pairs should read and re-read their work aloud to each other in turn with the listener responding constructively to support the writing.
Stories can then be illustrated and shared with the whole class.

A coat for a king

Session twelve:

Comparing stories

Before working with this story it will be helpful to collect together a basket of 'trickster tales' (such as those of Anansi or Brer Rabbit). These can be used as choices for a read aloud session or for children to browse and read together in paired or independent reading times.

Read the story aloud and share memories of other trickster tales. Together compile a list of famous tricksters in a 'rogues gallery' grid and including the usual suspects such as foxes or wolves alongside particular characters.
Discuss together the characteristics of the tricksters.
Do the children think they are all rogues? Is there anything to redeem any of them?

characters	stories	trick	comeuppance
Anansi			
foxes			
wolves			
Rumpelstiltskin			
Brer Rabbit			

I want my son!

Performance

Tell the children that they are going to perform this story as a group and record it onto a DVD. Making a 'performance for voices' in this way is a powerful way to help children to develop their understanding of story, language and structure.

Prepare a written version of the first part of the story up to 'bringing out her blushing daughter' and read it aloud together. Then discuss how you might read it aloud as a group to enhance enjoyment and understanding for the listener, sharing the reading between you. You might decide for example to read the narration as a whole group or as pairs, while individuals or small groups read in role as the different characters. Are there parts which should be shouted or whispered? Are there lines which could be repeated for effect? As you make each decision highlight and annotate the text.

Try out different ideas together before rehearsing and presenting it to another class or adult for their comment. Finally, record it as a disc or sound file.

Once children have worked in this way as a whole class they can go on to work as groups on other parts of the story.

Bookmaking

Read aloud the remaining two stories.
Ask the class to discuss their favourites from the whole collection and to give reasons for their choices. As a class compile a top three and then ask them to write another story themselves using similar characters, places and themes. Working with a writing partner, the children can go on to write their individual folk tales, sharing drafts and making helpful comments. These should then be illustrated in the style of the book, bound into a class anthology, and kept in the book area for everyone to enjoy.

Emily Gravett
Author Study

A teaching sequence of 5 to 6 weeks

Learning aims

- To read and engage in depth with a range of books by one illustrator/author

- To explore and interpret the way Emily Gravett draws and conveys meaning

- To encourage children to 'read illustration' critically and closely engage with it

- To develop children's own understandings of the ways in which they can use drawing to communicate meaning

- To encourage children to work in a multi-modal way to convey meaning

This chapter will focus on the work of prize-winning illustrator/author Emily Gravett and explore her original, distinctive and inventive style. In Emily Gravett's work every detail of the book has a part to play so that the whole is considerably more than its parts. Her illustrations are always clever, inventive and engaging, her language is strong and rhythmic, and she is the complete master of the surprise ending.

This author study will focus on three picture books, *Dogs, Meerkat Mail* and *Little Mouse's Big Book of Fears*. However, teachers will want to encourage children to explore and enjoy all of Emily Gravett's books to provide as many opportunities as possible for them to discover their own favourites among her extensive work.

Key Teaching Approaches

Booktalk

Shared writing

Bookmaking

Role-play

Information writing

Responding to illustration

Drawing

Writing and performing poetry

Hot seating

Re-enactment through play

Writing

Before beginning this unit:

Start by making a display, collecting together as many of Emily Gravett's books as possible but also including some of the songs, stories and traditional nursery rhymes that resonate through her books. Talk with children about what they already know about her and her books and tell them that they are going to find out as much as they can about this distinctive illustrator/author.

Session one:

Introducing Emily Gravett

Begin by exploring Emily Gravett's website together as a class. (**www.emilygravett.com**)

This is a clever and very child-friendly interactive website which is constantly changing and regularly updated. It contains a lot of information about

Emily Gravett herself including a video of her talking about her published and about to be published books. It also contains some playful activities that can be downloaded and are ideal for children to enjoy in class and at home. Once children have been introduced to the website ask them to work together in pairs to explore it and to make a list of five interesting facts about the author. Each pair should then join with another pair to share their lists and to decide a final list of the five most important facts. As a class, discuss each group's selections and decide on a final class list.

Session two:

Shared writing, biography

Using shared writing, write a biographical sketch of Emily Gravett drawing on the children's research.

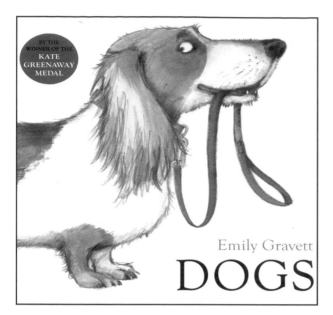

DOGS

A wonderfully satisfying book with a twist in the tail, this is a celebration of dogs and their individuality which sings out at you as you read it.

Booktalk and persuasive writing

Read the first two pages of *Dogs* aloud and tell the children that you want to see if they can read the book using only the pictures. Cue them in with "I love…" each time. Now read the whole book aloud, this time encouraging the children to use the pattern, the rhyme and the pictures to help them predict and join in as you do so. Re-read the book together, talking with the children about their favourite pages and discussing how we know what the words say from the ways in which Emily Gravett has drawn the pictures.

If you could choose to take one of the dogs home which one would you take and why?

Put children into pairs to argue the case for their chosen dog. Invite some children to present their argument to the rest of the class for the audience to guess which dog has been chosen. Children go on to draw their chosen dog and to write an advertisement to persuade someone to take it home.

Role-play

What sorts of things do the children think a dog would say about cats?
Invite children to go into role as dogs from the book and to come along and give their opinion about cats.

Shared writing

As a class, and using shared writing to help shape the children's ideas, write in role as a dog to make and illustrate a similar book about cats. Independent writers will enjoy writing their own versions, maybe from the perspective of another animal.

Writing an information text

Suggest children write their own information books about dogs choosing either a particular breed of dog, or one which has a particular job to do (such as a 'seeing' or 'hearing' dog). Some children might also choose to write about their own beloved pet. Provide children with a variety of information books and other resources to use for their research. As they write, encourage them to read their work aloud to a partner for comment. When the work is finished children should edit their work with the help of their partner before going on to rewrite their work into books that they have cut into the shape of the animal itself. When the books are finished, children should share them with another class before adding them to the class information resources for everyone to enjoy.

MEERKAT MAIL

Sunny the meerkat is feeling suffocated within the bosom of his loving and large family. He decides he needs to take a break away and sets off to explore the outside world and to make acquaintance with his extended family.

At each resting place he sends a postcard home describing his adventures. But, after a week away, he's only too happy to return home, having come to appreciate the blessings of a meerkat's home. This is an amusing story which emphasises the value of family and community. We are told much about what Sunny's relatives are like and how

Sunny feels about the places that he visits but little of this is spelt out for us. Instead the reader is left to 'read between the lines' and the book offers much scope for talking together about the ways in which Emily Gravett lets us know what Sunny thinks through her illustration and choice of words.

Sessions eight and nine:

Responding to illustration; Reading journal

Show the children the book itself, and the way it is packaged as if it was a parcel. Open it up together to discover the scrap book/photo album itself. Look at the endpapers and talk with the children about the sorts of things that they show and what they might suggest about what lies inside the book. Discuss with the children what they themselves would choose to include if they were making their own photo albums. Give each child an A4 landscape scrapbook to begin to decorate and collage in the same way as *Meerkat Mail* is personalised. This is going to be a personal reading journal for children to use as they work with this book. Suggest they bring photographs from home and other memorabilia to add to their own drawings and sketches.

Session ten:

Drawing and annotation

Read aloud the first three pages.
What do we learn about the meerkat family in these first pages?
Ask children to draw a meerkat and annotate it with all the things that they know about them.

Writing poetry

Ask the children what they know about the Kalahari desert and what they think it might be like before looking together at some images of it on the interactive whiteboard.
Show them slowly. As you do so ask the children to talk in pairs about what each image makes them think about, how it makes them feel, and whether it reminds them of anything.
Re-show the images and discuss responses as a whole class.

Focus on one image and ask the class to give you words which describe how the picture makes them feel and phrases to describe what they can see.

Begin to write a shared poem, deciding first on which word or phrase would make a strong beginning before going on to select words and phrases in turn from the list.

Explore the effect that repeating certain lines has. Children go to write their own poems either as individuals or as supported groups in guided writing.

Performing the poem

Put the children into groups to perform their poems. Suggest that they experiment with reading some lines of the poems in unison, some as individuals and some as paired voices.
Once they have performed their poems children write the poems in their 'best' handwriting into their journals and illustrate them.

Booktalk

Read aloud to the end of the book and ask the children to write into their journals what they think about the story using the 'Tell me' grid to help them focus on the things they have liked or not liked in it and any puzzles it has presented them with. When they have finished, talk with the children as a class about their responses, discussing aspects of book design as well as the story itself.

Plotting the story

Sunny's travels take him across Africa. Use the interactive whiteboard to look together at a geographical map of the continent and to work out where Sunny went using the clues from the postcards.

Drama and role-play

As a class, plan a trip around the country for Sunny using places that are special to the children and that they already know something about. Ask children to work in groups to choose one of these places and create a living tableau of the sort of picture that might be on a postcard a visitor might send. Each group in turn should then present these to the rest of the class. Take photographs to capture each group's work. Invite the audience to suggest words and phrases which describe what they think the place is like. Children go on to place their own photograph into their reading journal and write an accompanying description for it.

Researching and writing information

What do the children think Meerkats and their relatives are really like?

Talk with the class about what they think they know about meerkats, listing the things they know and identifying those things that they would like to find out more about.

Encourage children to work in a variety of groupings working in small groups, pairs or as individuals, and to take one or two questions that interest them to research and find out some answers for. Suggest they collect the information in a range of ways, sometimes making notes, sometimes drawing or annotating diagrams. As they work make time for children to talk and report back about the things they have discovered. Finally suggest children choose a way to present their information maybe as a poster, or a leaflet, or as a riddle book with the answers presented under flaps.

LITTLE MOUSE'S BIG BOOK OF FEARS

Emily Gravett has said that she created this book for those who like herself are afraid of everything. Every child will certainly be able to identify with the poor little mouse as he describes his fears within the pages of this book. As he does so, they will be able to explore their own fears whether it be a fear of creepy crawlies, of the dark or of falling into the toilet!

The book is presented from the outset as if it is the mouse's own personal journal with each page presenting the reader with a different text-type experience whether it be a cut out map, newspaper cuttings, handwritten scribbles or pop-ups. It is an ideal book for children to read both on their own or with adults.

Booktalk

Talk with the children about their responses to the cover of the book before watching Emily Gravett on the website of the book where she talks about how she conceptualised the book in the beginning and the lengths she went to in order to present the book as something that the mouse had eaten his way into.

Read the book aloud all the way through before talking with the children about their first responses to the book and returning to look more closely together at the pages which have been particularly memorable for some of them.

Booktalk and bookmaking

Which of the mouse's fears do the children most empathise with? Do they have secret fears of their own?

Suggest children make their own 'special' books which they can use to write or draw about the things that they worry about. Emphasise that nobody will read their book unless they want them to so children don't have to share their fears with anyone unless they choose to do so.

Look at the cover and design of *Little Mouse's Big Book of Fears* and talk together about what the children think it tells them about the mouse. Children go on to design the covers for their own books.

Responding to illustration

As a class list all the fears that the mouse has. Choose one of the fears from the list and talk with the children about why they think the mouse might be fearful of it.
Look together at the ways in which Gravett's illustrations and use of typography help us to understand more about the mouse and how the mouse is feeling.
Suggest children draw and annotate the mouse.

Hot seating and shared writing

Invite the children to go into role as the mouse to talk about the things that frighten him and how they make him feel.

Using shared writing write a class poem together about how the mouse feels using a beginning such as:

I'm afraid of everything I see

Suggest children use this as a repeating motif to help structure their ideas.
Children go on to write their own poems using this structure to shape their poem or by improvising their own beginning.
When they are finished, set time aside for them to work with a partner to rehearse and present it for the rest of the class's enjoyment before collecting them all together into a class book.

Session five and six:

Storyboxes

As individuals or in pairs children choose one Fear about which to make a storybox. For example, they might make a Creepy Crawlies box or a 'Things that go bump in the night' box. When they are finished children play with the boxes to make and tell scary stories together. Invite some children to share their story with the class or offer pre-prepared books in which they can write their stories.

Session seven:

Responding to illustration

Look together at the map of the 'Isle of Fright' and discuss how Emily Gravett uses it to show what the mouse feels when he is afraid. Draw a large outline of a person. Describe for the children how you feel and how you might show it when you are feeling apprehensive about something, for example,

'I bite my nails when I'm fretting about something…' annotating the drawing as you do so.

What do the children do when they are anxious about something?
Collect together other books that deal with anxieties and fears such as Cressida Cowell and Neal Layton's *Emily Brown and the Thing.* Set aside time to read and discuss these with the class.

Session eight:

Letter writing

Suggest children write a letter to advise the mouse using a combination of both drawing and writing. When the letters are finished children read them to each other before collecting them together in a class journal for everyone to read.

Session nine:

Booktalk and ICT

Revisit the display of Emily Gravett's work.

If the children could only choose one book from the collection which one would they choose and why?

Put the class into pairs to talk about their choices and to explain to each other what it is about this book that they particularly like or are drawn to. For example, are there particular pictures that they like or phrases or words that they enjoy? Bring the class back together and talk about the books together using a flipchart or interactive whiteboard notebook to help capture the children's responses.

Children go on to work in groups to make a presentation about their chosen book using powerpoint or smartboard applications. When they are finished each group presents their work to another class to encourage them to read the book themselves.

Acknowledgements

We thank the following:
For permission to use examples of their children's work in this book:

Sally Baines
The Betty Layward School, Hackney
Tim Souster
Edmund Waller Primary School, Lewisham
Mishelle Heckenburg
Arnhem Wharf Primary School, Tower Hamlets
Tina Chawla
Thornhill Primary School, Islington
Bernadette Ojobo
St James the Great RC School, Southwark
Davinia Leggett
The Hyde School, Barnet
Helen Billam
The Betty Layward School, Hackney
Ann Driscoll
Oliver Goldsmith Primary School, Brent
Mel Ahmet
Thornhill Primary School, Islington
Janice Lewis and **Karen Baldwin**
Deansfield Primary School, Greenwich
Kerry Gallagher
Tower Bridge Primary School, Southwark
Mayespark Primary School, Redbridge

For permission to use examples of their classrooms at work:
Thornhill Primary School, Islington
Edmund Waller Primary School, Lewisham

For their work:
Nick Price
Anne Forsyth

For kind permission to use illustrations

The Princess and the White Bear King
illustration © Nicoletta Ceccoli
Barefoot Books, 2004

Man on the Moon - a day in the life of Bob
illustration © Simon Bartram
Templar Publishing, 2002

Little Mouse's Big Book of Fears
illustration © Emily Gravett
Macmillan, 2007

Dogs
illustration © Emily Gravett
Macmillan, 2009

Meerkat Mail
illustration © Emily Gravett
Macmillan, 2006

A Fistful of Pearls and other tales from Iraq
illustration © Shelley Fowles
Frances Lincoln 2008

Grace & Family
illustration © Caroline Binch
Frances Lincoln 1995

Lila and the Secret of Rain
illustration © Jude Daly
Frances Lincoln 2007

Mia's Story
illustration © Michael Foreman
Walker Books 2006

Mufaro's Beautiful Daughters
illustration © Estate of John Steptoe
Puffin 1987

The Puffin Book of Fantastic First Poems
illustration © Ann Kronheimer
Puffin 1999